# Daily Living Through God's Grace

## God's Food for the Spirit

**DEBORAH HARRIS CHRISTOPHER**

Copyright © 2015, 2012, 2008, 2007, 2024 Deborah Harris Christopher.

All rights reserved. No part of this book may be reproduced, stored, or transmitted by any means—whether auditory, graphic, mechanical, or electronic—without written permission of both publisher and author, except in the case of brief excerpts used in critical articles and reviews. Unauthorized reproduction of any part of this work is illegal and is punishable by law.

ISBN: 979-8-89419-367-0 (sc)
ISBN: 979-8-89419-368-7 (hc)
ISBN: 979-8-89419-369-4 (e)

Library of Congress Control Number: 2015901133

Because of the dynamic nature of the Internet, any web addresses or links contained in this book may have changed since publication and may no longer be valid. The views expressed in this work are solely those of the author and do not necessarily reflect the views of the publisher, and the publisher hereby disclaims any responsibility for them.

THE EWINGS PUBLISHING

One Galleria Blvd., Suite 1900, Metairie, LA 70001
(504) 702-6708

"Daily Living through God's Grace"
is dedicated to the memory of my parents
Herman and Mary Harris,
who under the guidance of God taught me honesty
and integrity.

In all thy ways acknowledge him,
and he shall direct thy paths.

**Proverbs 3:6, KJV**

# Contents

*Epigraph* ......................................................................................... viii
*Preface* ............................................................................................ ix
*Acknowledgment* ............................................................................ x
*Introduction* ................................................................................... xi

## Chapter 1 Loves Inspiration

Love Is ............................................................................................. 2
Mother ............................................................................................. 3
From Rags to Riches ...................................................................... 4
Opposites ........................................................................................ 5
Daddy's little Girl .......................................................................... 6
Good Luck My Friend ................................................................... 7
Because I Love Me ......................................................................... 8
Because I Can't See You ................................................................ 9

## Chapter 2 Praise

Thanks ........................................................................................... 12
Forgiveness ................................................................................... 14
Farewell ......................................................................................... 16
Tears of Joy ................................................................................... 18
One Great Love ............................................................................ 20
Midnight Hour ............................................................................. 22

God Knows ..................................................................................................... 24
Grace in your Face ........................................................................................ 26
I Give Up ........................................................................................................ 28
Home .............................................................................................................. 30

## Chapter 3 Struggles

Finding Fault ................................................................................................. 34
The Poison ..................................................................................................... 36
Me Mentality ................................................................................................. 38
The Fist ........................................................................................................... 40
Prepare to fight ............................................................................................. 42
Perfection ....................................................................................................... 44
Don't Block .................................................................................................... 46
I'm Mad .......................................................................................................... 48
Calling All Saints .......................................................................................... 50
Choices ........................................................................................................... 52
Beaters ............................................................................................................ 56
Addictions ...................................................................................................... 58

## Chapter 4 Guidance

Current Events Saints .................................................................................. 62
When God Says No ...................................................................................... 64
The Spirit ....................................................................................................... 66
Free Love ........................................................................................................ 68
Trust God ....................................................................................................... 70

| | |
|---|---|
| Unspoken | 72 |
| The Pain of a Gain | 74 |
| Life's Treasure | 76 |
| Confession | 78 |
| Bitter or Better | 80 |
| A soul of Gold | 82 |
| A World of my Own | 84 |
| All Aboard | 86 |
| Be a Man | 88 |
| A Name | 90 |

## Chapter 5 Dedications

| | |
|---|---|
| A Mother's Love | 94 |
| I Love You | 95 |
| What is a Mother? | 96 |
| Time | 97 |
| Just Because | 98 |
| "Just Keep on Living" | 99 |
| Wellborn | 100 |
| What Makes me a Woman? | 101 |
| A Life Well Lived | 102 |
| *About the Author* | 106 |

# Epigraph

God spoke to me and I answered. My obedience to God changed my life.

# Preface

"Daily Living through God's Grace" is a book of poetry that is unlike many other poetry books. This book is easy to read, understand, and uplifts the spirit. "Daily Living through God's Grace" covers a wide range of thoughts, ideas, and feelings through a course of about sixteen years. During that time I was a wife and working mother who suffered from Depression and many other health conditions. It was during that period in my life that I realized that I could only depend of God for answers. This book expresses the many paths through my journey.

# Acknowledgment

First of all, glory to God for speaking through me for many years. God would speak to me to get out of bed or whatever else I was in the middle of and just write as if I was taking dictation. During that time, I got into the habit to always keep with me a pen and paper so I could write as the words, thoughts, and ideas came to mind. Once I realized that I created the poems I would just continue to write. I started to share the poems with family, friends, and co-workers who found the poems to be enjoyable. It was still many years to pass before the Lord spoke to me that the poems were not given to me to keep or just share with only a few people. The poem's creations were a result of my obedience and love for God as He spoke to my heart and changed my life. I would like to also acknowledge all the encouragement I received from my family and friends to create this book. To each of you from the bottom of my heart, thank you.

# Introduction

"Daily Living through God's Grace" is the result of my obedience to God's directions. Following those directions not only produced a book, but produced a new me. This book is a look into my journey from being very depressed to a happy and bold woman of God.

The book has five chapters and they all have significant meanings. Chapter one, titled Loves Inspirations, is a collection of poems that in some way or another has given me a lot of joy. They were written at different phases of my life; recalling love between spouses, parents, friends, and of course self-love.

Praise is the title for chapter two poems, and is among the first series of poems that were written. These poems of course are praises to our Lord. Ironically, these poems were written during a time that I was deeply depressed.

Struggles is the third chapter and it was written at a time that God was really working on me as I tried to do things for myself rather than rely on Him. This chapter focuses on different day to day struggles that we all deal with in life such as selfishness, jealousy, and being judgmental.

The poems in chapter four, titled guidance, are the poems that were a result of wisdom and Christian love that I developed through the years as I walked closely with God.

Dedications, the final chapter, is an unusual chapter name. The entire chapter is a collection of dedications to people who are or were very important and influential in my life.

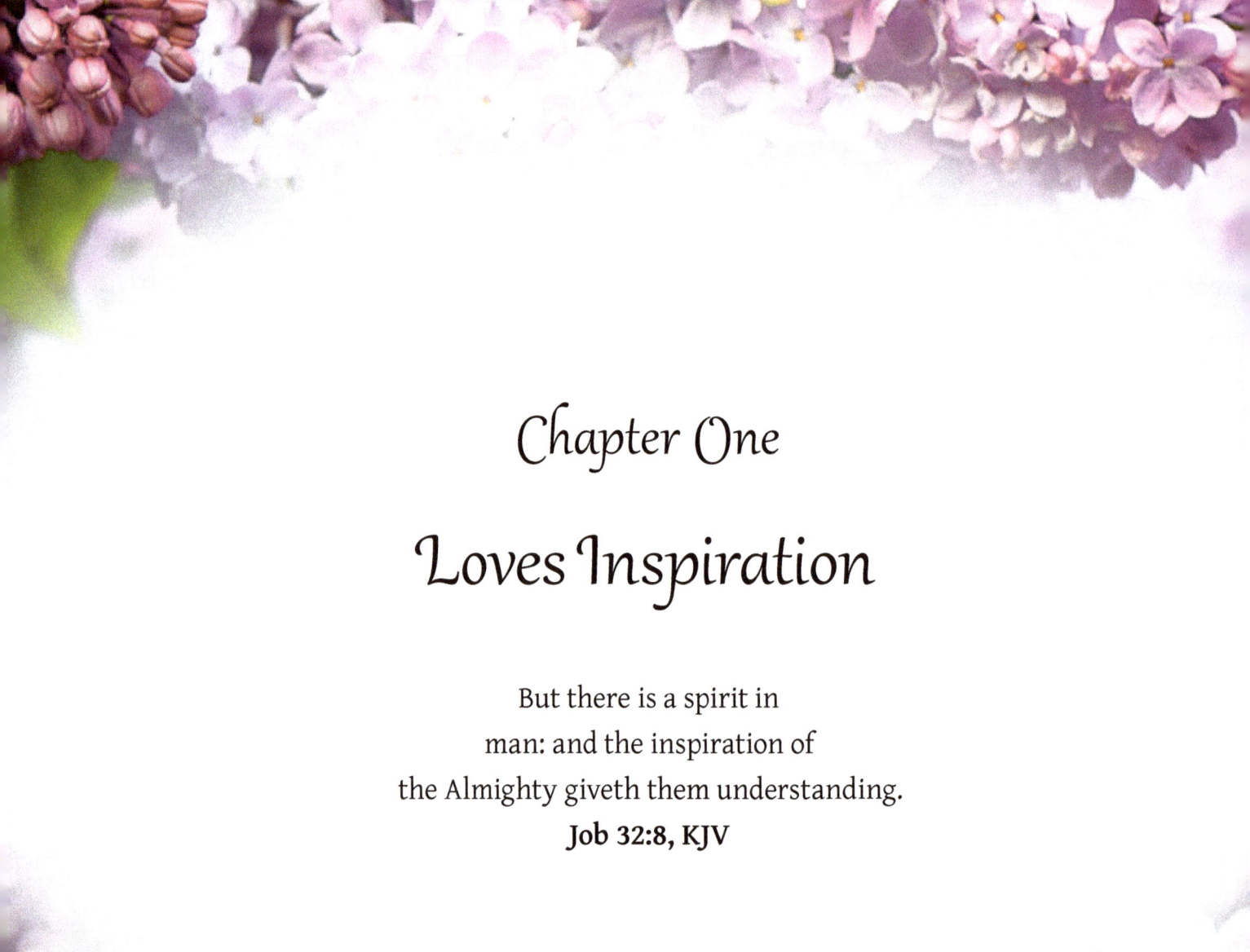

# Chapter One

# Loves Inspiration

But there is a spirit in
man: and the inspiration of
the Almighty giveth them understanding.
**Job 32:8, KJV**

# Love Is

Love is when waiting your turn
is no real concern.
It is when I will do anything for you
just because you're you.
Love is sacrifice
without thinking twice.
Because your relationship is at stake,
love is wanting to give and not take.

# Mother

There is not enough money
or objects to give
to ask you to forgive.
You did not have a easy life, but
through it all you were a
good mother and wife.
I can look to the north, south,
east, and west and know
that mom you are the best.
Although you were not a star,
because of your heart we all went far.
we are now most times apart,
but you will forever be in my heart.

# From Rags to Riches

I confessed Christ at age twelve. My parent's belief in God is something that I thank them for daily (living by example). Some things you can't learn in church, if you know what I mean. For years I went to Sunday school and church without really feeling what the goodness of God's glory was really all about. Yes, we were poor financially, but I did not realize that I was living in spiritual poverty. Today I am surely rich in the word and knowledge of God's love. Are you living in poverty?

# Opposites

Our lives together proves the fact
that opposites do indeed attract.
What others do not understand
can only come from God's command.
Not our love we always show, but
just as long as we both know.
There are days that I could cry, and
there are times that money can't buy.
Many said that it would not last, but
that's okay because together
we have a blast.

# Daddy's little Girl

He holds her tight in his arms
to keep her safe from all life's harm.
She is quite a beaut,
and can always get his loot.
No matter how much she whines, in her,
he only sees that the sun shines.
She is the apple of his eye,
his pearl in this world,
who else, but daddy's little girl.

# Good Luck My Friend

Good luck my friend.
Needless to say you are unlike the rest,
I do, however, wish you the best.
I can't say goodbye,
because it will just make me cry.
Good luck my friend is what I will say,
because it is hard to see you go away.
We've had long talks,
and now it is time for you to walk.
You have a good heart,
and that is always a great start.
One day we will see each other again,
and until then, I will say good luck my friend.

# Because I Love Me

Because I love me, I will:
Say no to drugs (pills and alcohol).
Say no to premature sex (STD's-HIV-babies).
Say no to smoking (bad for health).
Say no to gangs (die young).

Because I love me, I will:
Say yes to obeying my parents
(they love you-guidance).
Say yes to going to school (success).
Say yes to getting along with others
(live in society successfully).
Say yes to age appropriate things
(childhood is precious and once it's gone you cannot get it back).

Asking each and every child to first
love themselves.

# Because I Can't See You

Because I can't see you, my best
days are bitter sweet.
My love for you will never end,
years later, still hard to comprehend.
I can't see you because you are
no longer here.
Thoughts deep in my heart will
keep you near.
Because I can't see you,
my whole life is blue.
I can't see you,
but I can think of you.
Fond memories from the past,
stitched in my memory to forever last.

All scripture is given by inspiration
of God, and is profitable for doctrine,
for reproof, for correction, for instruction
in righteousness:
**2 Timothy 3:16, KJV**

# Chapter Two

# Praise

By him therefore let us
offer the sacrifice of praise
to God continually, that is,
the fruit of our lips giving
thanks to his name.
**Hebrews 13:15, KJV**

# Thanks

When you have a special ability
you must maintain humility.
It's not hard to see
God is good to me.
God gives us humility to keep us grounded
when things are going good.
He wants to teach us perseverance
when things are going bad.
We must have balance
in order to overcome life's challenges.
So when God blesses you,
just simply say thank you.

Jesus is coming back that is a fact.

# Forgiveness

We do not always do as we should,
or even what we could.
Even when you fall, you can always call.
He's open twenty-four hours a day to help you find the way.
So get back on track,
He will always take you back.
So as you walk away from sin, remember
He will forgive you, again, and again.

Brand new mercy and grace allows
me one more day to face.

# Farewell

It's hard to say goodbye to
someone you love,
they've gone to a better
place to be with God above.
When it's your loved one He takes,
remember God does
not make mistakes.
Although you may have
loved them since birth,
remember God loved them first.
Your loved one is gone, and may they rest,
but it's God almighty, who loved them best.

He will give you grace
and run your race.

# Tears of Joy

Tears of joy is something
that anyone can employ.
You may think that I am sad,
but in reality, I know that I am glad.
At times I just sit and cry,
not because I'm sad, or hurt,
but knowing that
God' grace and mercy has
not passed me by.

He will be your shelter in times of bad weather.

# One Great Love

My one great true love,
who else, but the heavenly Father above.
You are the love of my life,
although I am someone else's wife.
You have done so much for me,
whatever is your will I know that it will be.
You made me what I am today,
so as a salute of thanks,
I will continue to pray, pray, and pray.

It's quite simple, there are no flaws in God's Temples.

# Midnight Hour

Right now there is no spark,
yes it's totally dark.
I don't mean Georgia Power,
I'm referring to the midnight hour.
But that's okay because I have a
spirit guide to light the way.
Stay focused on the light,
it's great to know there is a
loving guide who will help
you see in the midnight.
Dear Lord, I know I don't have to sigh,
because you will keep
your beams on high.
From the start
you must do your part.
During this time you must stay around
by standing your ground.
Remember not to fear,
and take off running, because after
all joy comes in the morning.

Self-Love comes from the knowledge of God above.

# God Knows

When you know it's not right,
but you can no longer fight.
God Knows!
Though you've been wronged,
you still must stay strong.
Always do your best,
and let God take care of the rest.
God sees all, knows all,
and is always there to catch
you when you fall.
Remember before you went through,
God already knew.

What a debt, what a fine, to lay down your life for all mankind.

# Grace in your Face

Of me you may not think much,
it just took Jesus' hand for me to touch.
When man sees me,
it's only my past he seems to see.
You can't put me in heaven or hell,
so what business is it of yours to tell?
Judging me is not your job,
so when you talk about me,
why should I sob?
A true Christian will understand,
no man is worthy of His hand.
So I will openly praise Him
and forget the chatter,
for God's love and
understanding is the
only thing that matters.
And if you still don't understand,
I will make the command,
To say "God's grace in your face".

Don't cry for me because
I have been set free.

# I Give Up

Trying to make things right,
worrying about it day and night.
Wrong to continue until
nothing else is left,
I give up because I will no longer
try to do it by myself.
Christ carried the cross of burden so
we did not have to.
So tell me why, why, we continue to.
I give up sounds like words of despair,
but are in fact words of repair.

We are the light of the world so let our beacons shine in spite of the world.

# Home

Home is that special place where
I always feel the warmth of
love, kindness, and peace.
Unfortunately, some in life
never really feel that love and
peace in their earthly home.
But, praise God, there is a
heavenly home, waiting for all who
love and obey the Lord.
It is sad to think that simple
things we often take for granted is
not enjoyed by everyone.
I am truly blessed to have a
earthly home of peace.

A place I am always happy and
anxious to return.
My refuge from the world
and all its problems.
Home is that very special place
of love and peace of mind.
Some will enjoy most of our earthly
days and then continue in heaven.
Sadly, there are others who will
enter that special place of peace
where they had never been,
until the very end.

God's greatest gift of all is He's still there when we fall.

And thou shalt love the Lord thy God with all thine heart, and with all thy soul, and with all thy might.

**Deuteronomy 6:5, KJV**

# Chapter Three

# Struggles

For where envying and strife
is, there is confusion
and every evil work.
**James 3:16, KJV**

# Finding Fault

A question we often ask is whose fault is it?
Whose fault is it when I'm not happy?
Whose fault is it when I get in trouble?
Whose fault is it when I don't do what
I am supposed to do?
The answer to the question is simple.
Just ask another question.
Who is the one, and only person
responsible for me?
It is of course me.

Hate will keep you out of the gate

# The Poison

Poison is a substance that causes a disturbance. Not good to look at, or good to be around. It leaves a bitter taste, and makes you frown. Being around poison is no fun, it can even make you want to run. Poison is unpleasant, and can cause negative reactions. The substance is dangerous, it can hurt you, and even be lethal. Yet we continue to expose ourselves to poison. Christians should always be careful of poisonous exposure. Just like a bomb, we usually sit there as it continues to tick, and tick away in an explosion that could forever take us away.

Liar, Liar, will get you in fire.

# Me Mentality

The me mentality is all about me,
not helping anyone, not even family.
The word is selfish, and
when you are selfish,
not much will you accomplish.
You come into this world,
and leave it alone,
but in living you can't do it on your own.
Life is about give and take,
and without giving,
there's not much of an
impression you will make.

To get it right,
get Satan out of sight.

# The Fist

The fist balled tight,
careful to not let anything out.
Busy to not let go of anything,
but also blocking a way to get something.
The fist all nice and tight,
determined not to do what's right.

Not serving God is not a gamble,
your life will surely be in a shamble.

# Prepare to fight

Life is hard and full of stress,
but just the same we should do our best.
Satan, Satan, I must confess,
I no longer want to be a part of your mess.
When things go wrong,
we must be strong.
Keep your thoughts, and actions pure,
or Satan will get you for sure.
He will use any, and everything as bait,
so don't just sit back and wait.
Make plans for your escape,
so you can make it to the heavenly gates.
This is a war we all have to fight.
So put on God's armor, and prepare
to fight both day and night.

Don't wait until you die to figure out Satan is a lie.

# Perfection

Perfection, none of us have it, but we can
all make the connection.
We all strive for it,
but none really survive it.
We constantly insist on perfection in our lives.
The more we love the more pressure,
the kind that no human can
be successfully measured.
Perfection is a word we often use,
one that can easily confuse.
The definition of perfection is
completeness, and flawlessness.
Can a human really be complete
with no flaws?
We seem to think so with our actions and thoughts.
We made mistakes, but is it so hard to see
our loved ones do the same.
Perfection of some sort is wanted by
every soul, but in reality is an
unattainable goal.

Don't be bound, Jesus can help you to higher ground.

# Don't Block

Don't block your blessing,
it's the ultimate lesson.
Some people never learn,
therefore, they can never earn.
When you do little things when
no one is looking, and just
because it's right,
God will bless you openly with big things.
So always do what is right,
It will certainly come to light.

So full of the world, so empty inside.

# I'm Mad

I'm mad, I'm mad,
so mad that I can't see.
Oh what, Oh what could
the source of my anger be.
In theory, we can take this here,
there, and everywhere.
I don't like this, I don't like that,
always unhappy is a known fact.
After many years of soul searching
became the reality,
the real source of my anger is me.

Enjoy, don't destroy your temple.

# Calling All Saints

All you saints of the world,
I don't mean to be nosy,
I don't mean to prod,
but in times of trouble, do
you always go to God?
Had a bad day, can't wait
to get to the phone,
instead of where you should be,
which is at the throne.
In Jesus I found a friend in whom I can really depend.
A friend such as He, you can't beat. You can tell Him your
secrets and never hear it again in the streets.
My friend can be your friend; all you have
to do is let Him in. As Christians, we know that we are in this
world, but not of this world. When the world goes wrong,
we must be strong. Everyone knows that in times of trouble
a true saint will not faint.
Saints have an obligation to preach and to teach.
You don't have to be book smart,
instead, you should have a good heart.
So I'm calling all saints to practice what you preach,
because if my life is in ruins, how can I teach?

Living in haste is such a waste.

# Choices

Life is a smorgasbord.
We all have a multitude of choices to make
through our lifetime.
Life choices can be as small as
what to wear?
Or as big as should I end my marriage?
Choices are things that we have to live with
and can be very serious.
The making of choices has
a tendency to show patterns.
You see a person who practically
lives on the streets,
staying here and there,
they are on drugs and doing
whatever it takes to make it
through the day.
Some may say that individual
Is a bad person.
That may or may not be true.

One thing for sure is that they
made a string of bad choices.
That string may have gone back as far as
what they decided to wear to school one day.
In turn, made them attract
a certain group of people.
Next, is the decision to continue
to engage yourself with people who,
how should I say this? Are not
"morally correct".
Then comes the decision to go along with
the crowd and do drugs.
Of course, it starts small and you think
it is really not going to hurt anyone.
From there you graduate to hard stuff.
Choices from there can continue
to go downhill.
The point is that this continuous pattern
does not have to go on.

God may allow individuals with bad
characters to come into your life,
but this does not mean you were to form
a relationship with that person.
The purpose of the meeting could have
been entirely different from the outcome.
At any given time that person could choose
to stop, and do the right thing.
From there you ask what is the right thing?
It's really quite easy.
Pray, and ask God for forgiveness.
Make and keep God first, and foremost
in your life.
Ask for guidance, wisdom, and
obey God's word.
So what are you going to do?
It's your choice.

His love will keep you together through all kinds of weather.

# Beaters

They all want something in
exchange for nothing
whenever possible.
Because you must give in order to receive
from God, they never really
become successful.
They are the beaters.
To be true, unless it's you,
you know one, and
have even encountered one.
We call you beaters because
you strike us forcefully, and repeatedly.
Never giving, always
taking as much as possible.
No consideration for my needs,
to you, I'm only a open hand
to fulfill your needs.

Enemies you must ignore, be an eagle, and continue to soar.

# Addictions

Addictions are sometimes
unseen afflictions.
They are the temporary
fixes for life's problems.
No one is exempt,
you have yours, and I have mine.
Addictions can ruin your life.
The whole day is consumed by trying
to feed the need of the addiction.
Whether it's gambling, smoking,
drugs, or overeating,
the costs can not only be monetary,
but also bring about physical,
or social demise.
You will have to be wise, addictions
often come in disguise.

O Lord, be gracious unto us;
we have waited for thee:
be thou their arm every morning,
our salvation also in the
time of trouble.
**Isaiah 33:2, KJV**

My child, just look into
the mirror and smile.

# Chapter Four

# Guidance

For this God is our God for
ever and ever: he will be our
our guide even unto death.
**Psalm 48:14, KJV**

# Current Events Saints

Saints you can't fight if you don't
realize there is a war.
Do you only concern yourself with
what goes on in the church?
Don't get me wrong, always praise
God, and give Him thanks.
But we must always know what is
going on in the world.
A lot of prophesized
bible events have began to surface
showing the end of times.
Time has started to come to an end.
If you don't believe it, just look at the signs.
The more you know about what's going
on in the world the more you'll know the need to pray.
We are living in the worst times
of most of our lives.
Prayer, along with knowledge is
the only way to really survive.

Sin will make your armor of glory thin.

# When God Says No

When God says no,
there is nowhere else to go.
When you know God,
you know the answer to your prayer.
You know if the answer is yes, no,
or not yet.
Part of faith is believing and trusting in
the answer to our prayer.
So when God says no,
there is nowhere else to go.
You can roam around in disbelief,
but it will only bring you more grief.

# The Spirit

Although your loved one is gone,
their spirit will live on.
The body is temporary,
but their spirit continues to live
forever inside of you.
One thing to understand is that
nothing can erase the soul
of a man/woman.
You will never forget they're gone,
but always remember their
spirit will live on.

Don't seal your fate by waiting too late.

# Free Love

Man says that nothing in life is free.
But that is not so.
Why?
Because the bible tells me so.
The love of God is free to both you and me.
His love is free to receive,
you need only to believe.
He is so wonderful, it is hard to conceive,
just walk in his path, and
heaven you will achieve.

Live in the world, not for the world

# Trust God

When you are sad and lonely, and don't know what to do,
ask God, trust Him, He will guide you through.
When the pain is so bad, and all you
can do is cry,
God is the one you should try.
You go to the doctor, you go to your friends,
but it is God who is in control at the end.
You say you love Him,
so trust Him.
Have the trials of the world got you down?
You don't have to be bound,
trust God, He is always around.
You know where to go, just get down on your knees,
you don't even have to say please.
We must continue to trust God, whether
things are going good, or bad, if you are happy or sad.
Continue to trust Him each and every day,
there is nothing more to say,
but trust God, trust God, and continually pray.

Don't take flight,
stay focused on the light.

# Unspoken

They say that action speaks
louder than words.
The things we do have more to do with
our spirit than what we say.
Your mouth can say anything,
but your actions, body
movements, and gestures will
speak for themselves.
This is because as we all know the talk
is a lot easier than the walk.
When dealing with people we should
always use our senses.
What we see is a lot more
powerful than what we hear.
Be wise,
and don't be fooled by the disguise.

When life becomes too hard to face, invite God to run your race.

# The Pain of a Gain

Before you succeed or make progress,
Satan is always there with his mess.
He keeps you bound,
and tries to turn you around.
It never fails, before there is success,
you will experience some pain.
The more it hurts,
the higher the worth.
Life is hard, and nothing comes easy.
Just remember before your gain,
you will feel some pain.

To stay strong, remain fixated on the throne.

# Life's Treasure

Don't build your life around
earthly treasures.
You will find it too hard to measure.
Material things are a
reflection of the flesh.
To fully succeed in life we must build up
spiritual treasures, instead of things
that bring about physical pleasure.
Pleasures of the flesh are only temporary,
but spiritual treasures will
bring you everlasting life.

Don't stray to the left or right, keep the throne in your sight.

# Confession

When you are wrong, you
are the first to know.
Why?
Because your conscience will tell you so.
Everyone experiences some sort
of sin, or wrong doing.
As long as we are in this world,
we will make mistakes, and do wrong.
Sometimes our wrongs may be deliberate,
and sometimes not.
Errors are often made, and we would
not be human if we didn't make them.
Just the same, we should own up
to our life's responsibility.

I'm sorry is sometimes two of the most
difficult words to say.
However, you should confess your
sins, and begin anew.
Carrying guilt is a heavy load,
and difficult to bear.
Confessing is a way of cleansing your soul
to go on, and do better.
They say that confession is
good for the soul.
It can also be important in
achieving life's goal.

# Bitter or Better

When things are not going well it is
easy to be bitter.
But we do have a choice,
we can choose to stay bitter,
or pray that things will get better.
This is a choice, not a destiny.
The reality is that we can be
what we want to be.
Happiness is yours to reach.

Touch the master's hand;
He will understand.

# A soul of Gold

A soul of gold can be under
no man's control.
There's no need to console,
because you have to be bold.
It may sound cold,
but the Devil it loathes.
The fruits of the spirit you must uphold,
so make it your life's goal
to have a soul of gold.

Be strong by leaving it at the throne.

# A World of my Own

I must stay in a world of my own,
because I know that I am God owned.
True, I must live in the world,
but the world does not have to live in me.
Through the world, Satan tries to bribe you,
but you must ask the Lord to
guide you.
Ask yourself?
Do you want to please God?
Or do you want to please the world?
The problems of the world
is that not enough
people want to please God,
they would rather please man.
Because after all,
no one can lie like Satan can.

Recognize you are God's seed
and you will not be in need.

# All Aboard

All aboard,
Next stop,
Heaven!
There is a train passing
through your town,
it's destination, heaven!
The ride is long, and it is on a straight,
and narrow path.
The ticket is free to all.
The conductor is Jesus,
who has gone along the same
path many years ago.
He continues to make the ride with
anyone would like to make the trip.
He is accompanied by the Holy Spirit
who acts as a Pullman porter to keep you
as comfortable as possible during the
tedious journey.
So all aboard, who's coming aboard.
Many will stop and get off
the train to enjoy
the sights of the world.
Some will get back on board again.
But who really knows?
The train may reach your destination
while you're at a rest stop.
Get on board, and stay on board.
We may just get there
sooner than you think.

Look to His face and get some grace.

# Be a Man

Be a man like only you can.
No one looks at a baby boy, and
says he is going to grow up to
be a drug dealer, child molester,
rapist, or gigolo.
The expectations are high,
and should remain high.
High expectations do require
a lot of work.
Growing up without the proper
father figure can make a boy a
man or a fool.
Young men you must break the cycle.

There is no excuse to spiral down
society as the image of a respectable
man becomes a myth.
To be a man, one must first love
God, and himself.
If you can achieve these two things,
then the task is easy.
Life situations can make this task easier
for some than others,
but nonetheless, can still be achieved.

This is a challenge to all young men and
boys, to Love God and himself.

Need a blessing?

Be a blessing.

# A Name

What does your name say
to the world?
Your name, your label for life.
Identifies who you are, and can
help determine who you will be.
Names effect how you are greeted,
or even perceived.
It can be a crutch, or an obstacle,
a strength, or a weakness.
A name can be the most precious gift
to give, or receive.

In every thing give thanks: for this is the will of God in Christ Jesus concerning you.
**1 Thessalonians 5:18 KJV**

When you live for God, the world will resent the Devil out of you.

# Chapter Five

# Dedications

But speaking the truth in love,
may grow up into him in all things,
which is the head, even Christ.
**Ephesians 4:15, KJV**

# A Mother's Love

As you lay soft in my tummy,
awaiting the first day you will
call me mommy.
I will rock you to sleep at night,
teach you the difference
between wrong and right.
Although there is no formal test,
I pray to do my very best.
A mother's job is never done,
I will be there for you,
from dusk to dawn.
Send praises to God in whose
love we can both smother,
I'll thank Him, thank Him,
for making me your mother.

Dedicated to my son Ethan Garrett Christopher

# I Love You

I love you no strings attached,
one thing for sure
is that we've got each other's back.
We have shared good times, bad times,
we have been through it all.
Admittedly, it has not always been a ball.
The more I needed you the more you made
your love shine through.
Without you I don't know where I would be,
words cannot express what it
feels like to know that you
are still here for all the world to see.

Dedicated to my husband Ralph B. Christopher, Jr.

# What is a Mother?

Who on earth can love you like no other?
Why of course that would be your mother.
God made mothers to be here on earth
to help to take away some of life's hurt.
Your mother is your nurturer, teacher,
cook, and seamstress.
Always there for you doing her best.
Mom's your number one fan,
she will get up and scream
for your victory
at a game like no one else can.
When others may get upset
with you and complain,
your mother is there with encouragement
to say "that's my baby" she would explain.
Her prayers will guide you whether
you are in or out of her sight,
there for you in time to make things right.
Ready to step in at any time when
you're in need.
I do this because I love you,
not necessarily,
because you are my seed.

Dedicated to the memory of
my mother Mary Harris

# Time

Time will take care of everything
a phrase you would use for
almost everything.
Often when it was used,
I, at times would be a little confused.
But as time went by,
I no longer had to ask why.
Time will take care of everything,
was your way of saying not to worry
about what tomorrow will bring.
You were always a good man, who gave
gave me faith and courage to live each day.
Time, that which is endless, and priceless,
can never be fully contained by us.
Never do we know what life will bring,
but I do know that time will take care of everything.

Dedicated to the memory of
my father Herman Harris

# Just Because

It is not because you are one of the most
handsome sights I've ever seen,
not just because you make my life gleam.
Not just because of what you've done,
not even because you're the only one.
I love you because you're you.
I know that together, whatever,
we will all make it through.
It's just because I love you, can't you see,
no matter what, unconditionally.

Dedicated to my nephew
Thomas Derrell Simon

# "Just Keep on Living"

By now she was gray, although you can tell
very beautiful in her day.
Very wise, almost a prophet in disguise.
She taught me many things about people,
and the world we live in.
Because the world is not kind,
pay them no mind.
Why should you care about something as simple as hair?
The color of skin has nothing to do
with the soul within.
When you are young there are many things you cannot believe,
or even conceive. Many a times when I was in doubt, my grandmother would
stop and shout "just keep on Living", a reality I still see each day.

Dedicated to the memory of
my grandmother Lizzie Wellborn.

# Wellborn

We all loved you so very much,
it was easy, your heart was so
easy to touch.
You were well known for your
boisterous laugh,
but sadly that was only the half.
A life so difficult we could only imagine.
You continued to have a good spirit
that could not be outdone.
Many things about you
we did not understand,
because it was only for us to
put in the Master's hand.
A much loved person who always
sat in the shadows of the family.
Until we lost you we really could not see.
You left us so suddenly, and it hurt so bad,
that day is easily recalled as one the
worst we've ever had.
Some comfort came shortly
after you left us.
I could clearly hear my
Grandmother say
"Wellborn" in a delightful way,
as if to say, I'm glad to see you and forever
to be with you and our Lord.

Dedicated to the memory of
my uncle Richard Wellborn

# What Makes me a Woman?

What makes me a woman?
What makes me a woman is the inner me,
that which you cannot see.
It certainly is not the amount of
physical love I share,
or the fruit I bear.
I am full of love, dignity, and grace,
which starts from within my
own inner space.

Dedicated to the many women I know who did not
sacrifice their dignity for the world.

# A Life Well Lived

He was strong, confident, and had a love
for life. An inspiration for some who
called him champ, but to me he was daddy.
Daddy's life was a life well lived.
Although his life was good,
it was hard to see him go.
Family as we know it will be no more.
A comfort to know he will
once again be with his wife.
The love of his life for fifty-four years.
As God willed them to be
together forever.
A life well lived, that which
no man can steal, and only for
God to give.

Dedicated to the memory of my father Herman Harris
and the love of his life, my mother
Mary Harris. Their love continues to last
Forever.

So then faith cometh by hearing,
and hearing by the word of God.
**Romans 10:17, KJV**

Righteous living is
a daily choice. What
do you choose?

A testament to my faith began when I could not have a child of my own. Although there were options, I chose to accept God's fate for me, whatever it would be. I learned to be content and accepted that I may never have a child. During that time came the realization that having a child would not make me a woman. Shortly after the birth of my son and being grateful to God for His blessing, I became ill. There were many times that doctors did not have an answer for me, and I fell into a deep depression. It was during this depression that my journey began.

# About the Author

Deborah Harris Christopher was born February 14, 1961 in Columbus, Georgia to the parentage of Herman and Mary Harris. She has two sisters, Loretta Simon and Gwendolyn Debro. Deborah confessed Christ at an early age, and has always openly expressed her love for God. On June 4th 1988, she married Ralph B Christopher, Jr., they reside in Byron, Georgia. Deborah is the mother of one son Ethan Garrett Christopher. She has two step-daughters Bisceglia Ferguson, and Shaquisha Lowe and five grandchildren. She is a deaconess and member of Saints in Praise (COGBF) ministries in Byron, Georgia under the pastoral guidance of Elder Wallace Porter Jr. and church Founder Elder Eddie Robinson, Sr.

"Daily Living through God's Grace" was written during a sixteen year period when Deborah is deeply depressed and experiencing many other health conditions. Although this was a very difficult period in her life, she still answered the call from God to write and record the many difficulties and pleasures during that time. This book is a product of the struggles, guidance, and praise to God that she endured during that time. "Daily Living through God's Grace is Deborah's answer to God as she uses poetry to minister to the world.

www.ingramcontent.com/pod-product-compliance
Lightning Source LLC
LaVergne TN
LVHW072126060526
838201LV00071B/4983